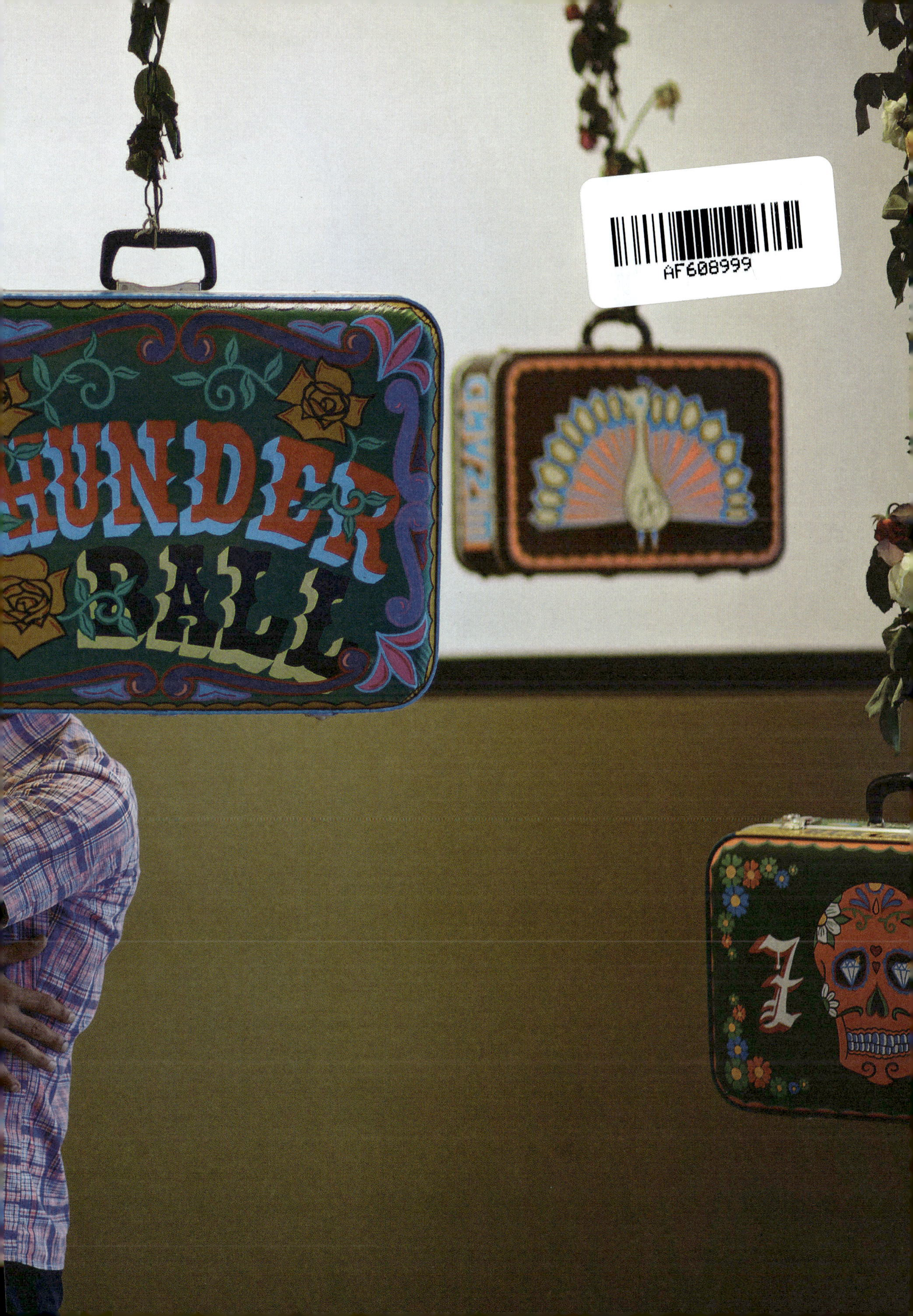
HUNDER
BALL
7

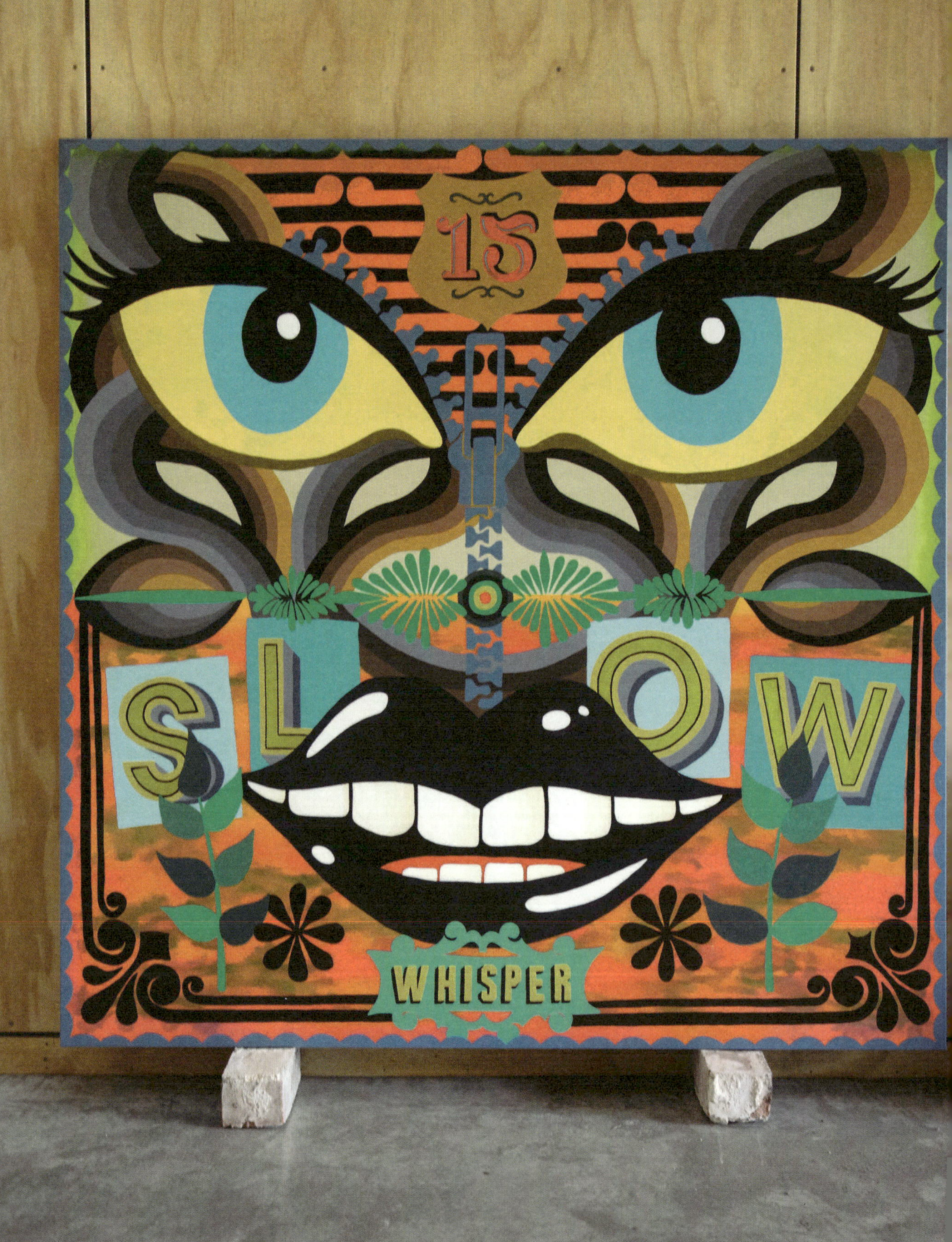
15
SLOW
WHISPER

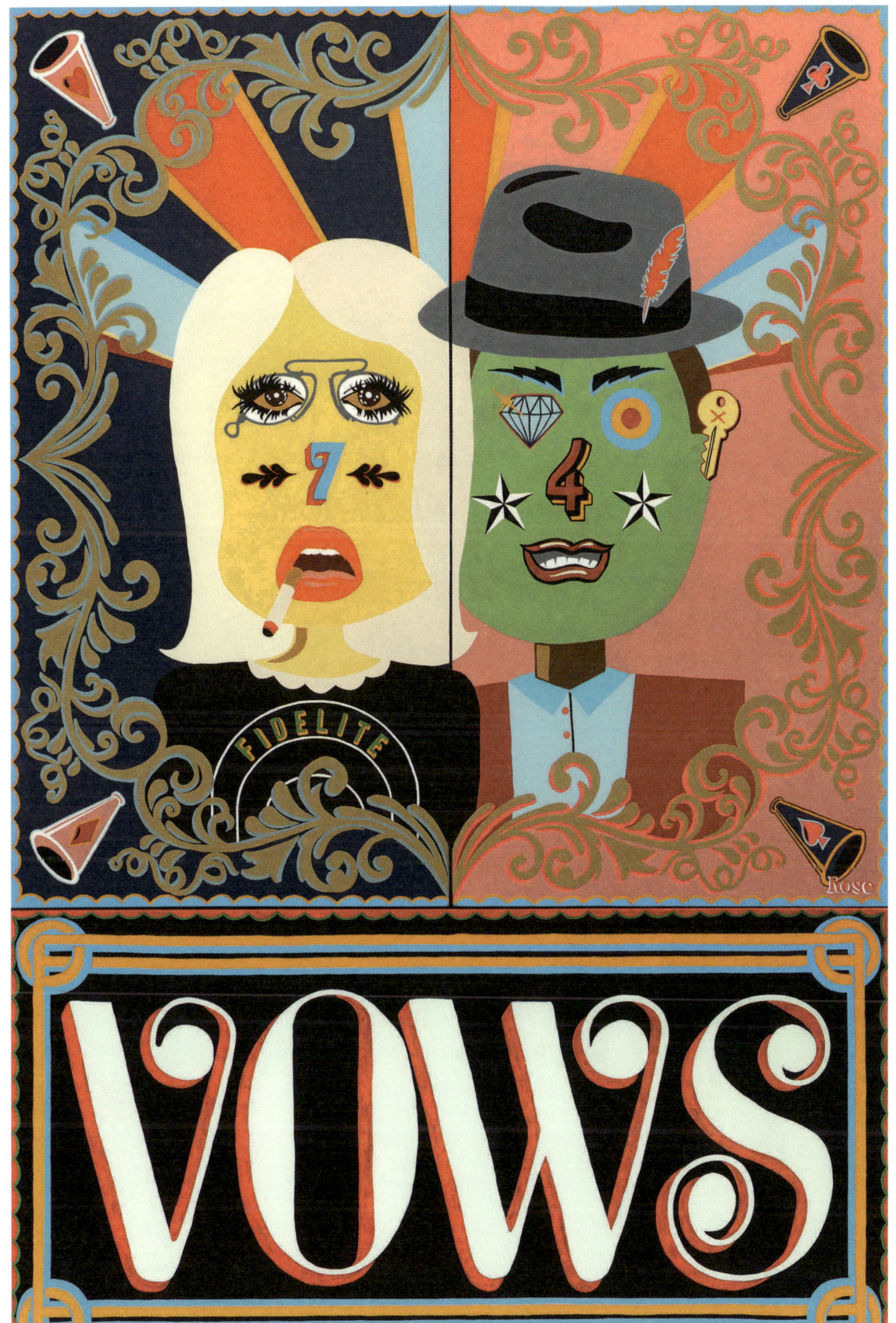
FIDELITE
Rose
VOWS

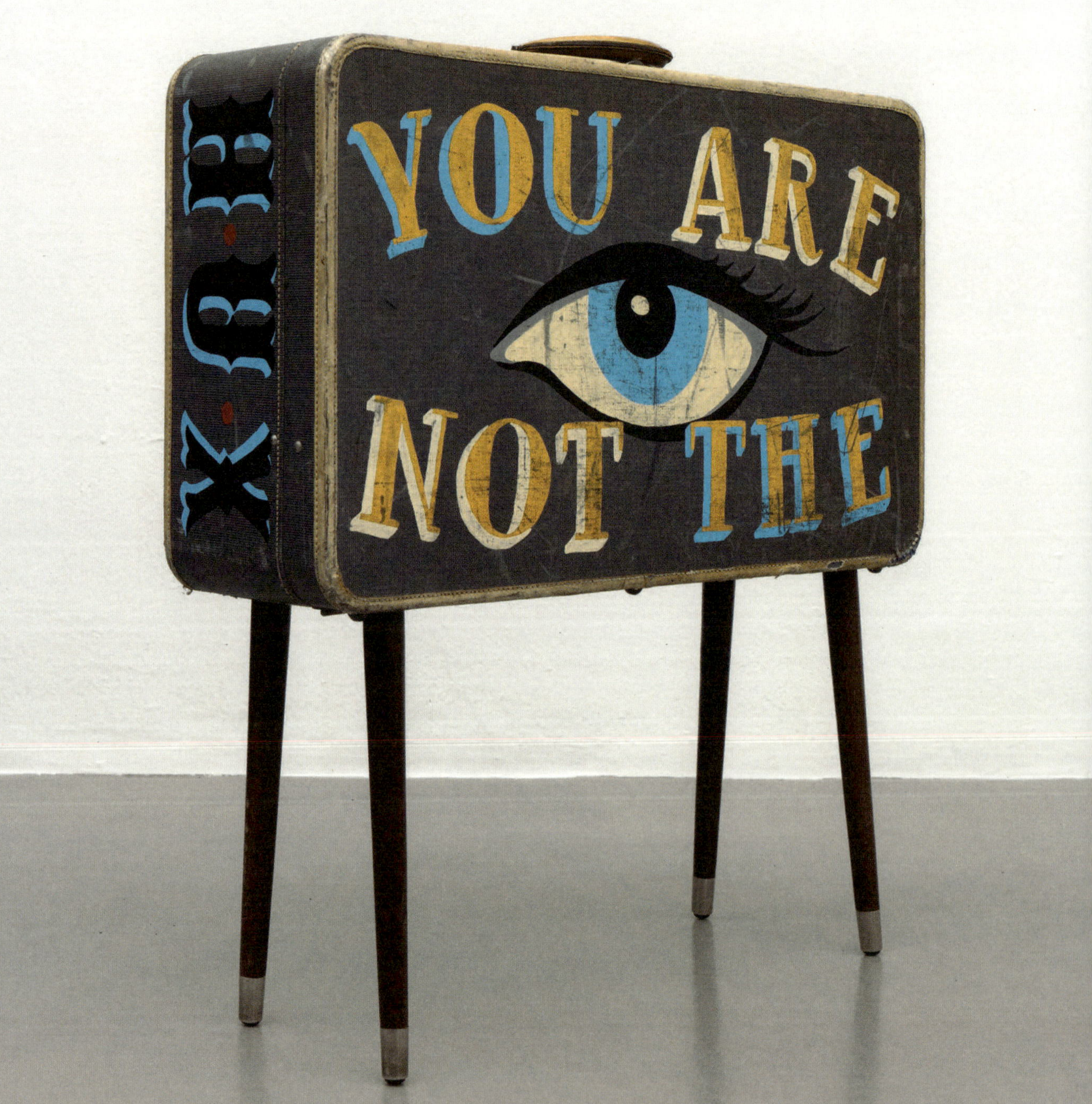
YOU ARE
NOT THE

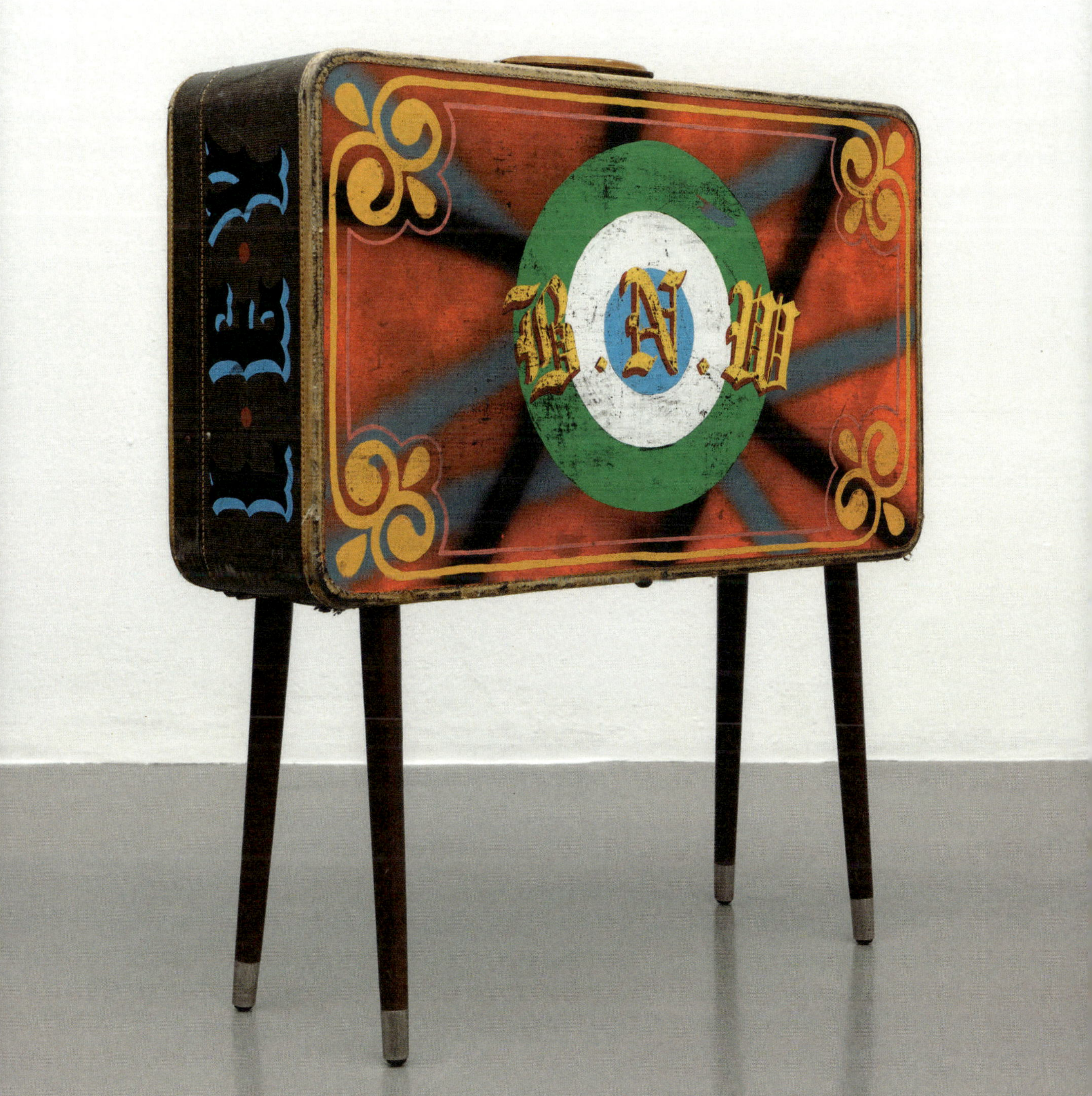
B.N.W

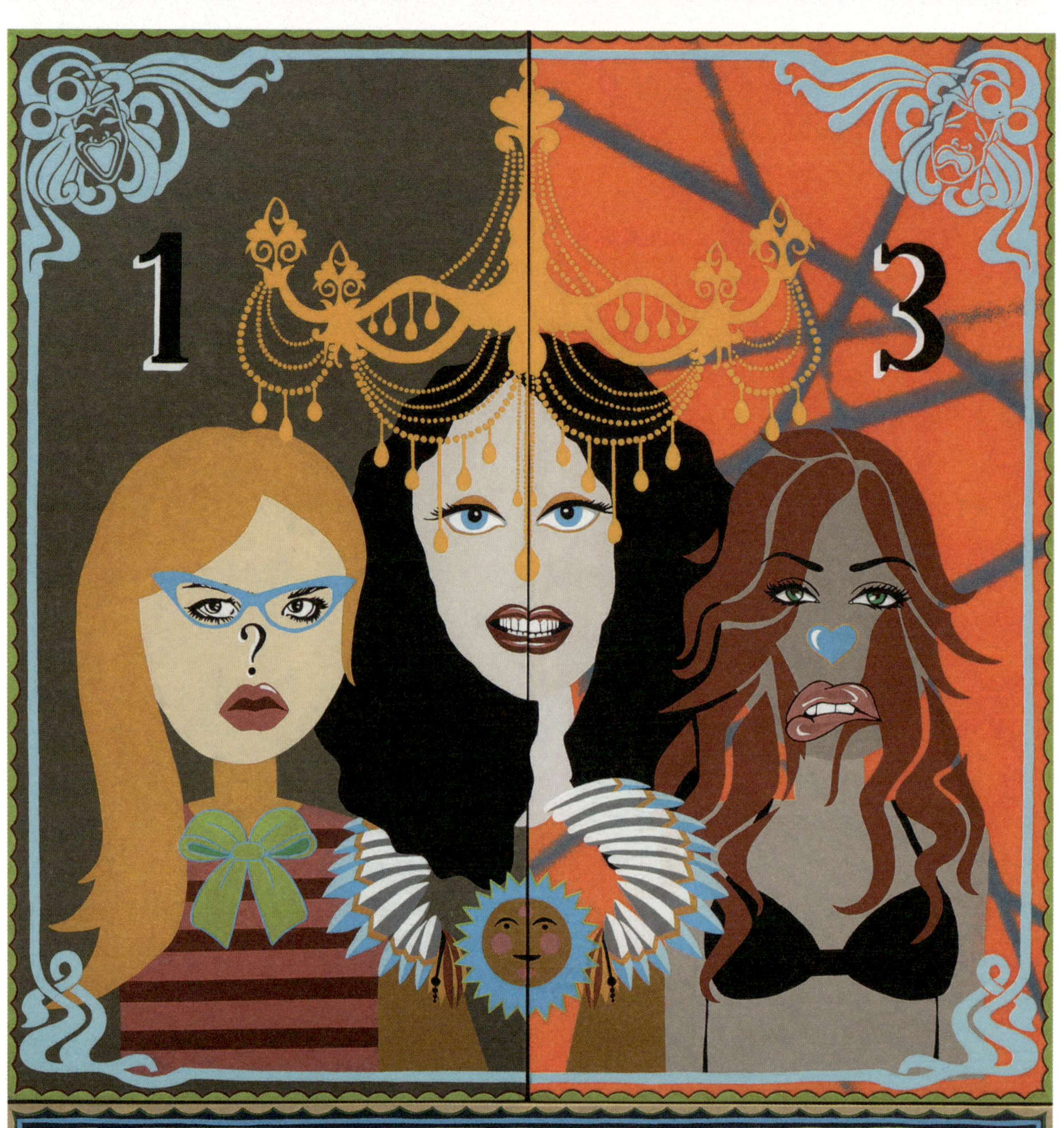

CONUNDRUM

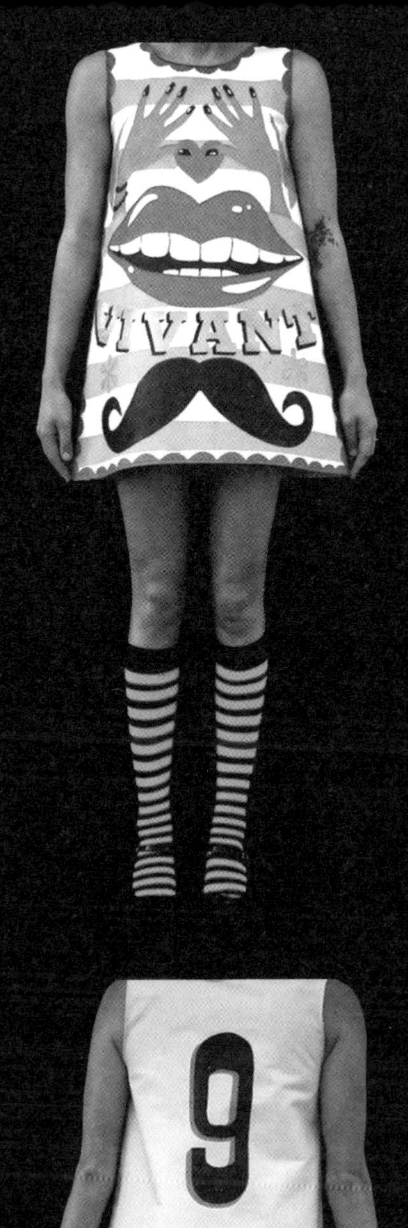
VIVANT

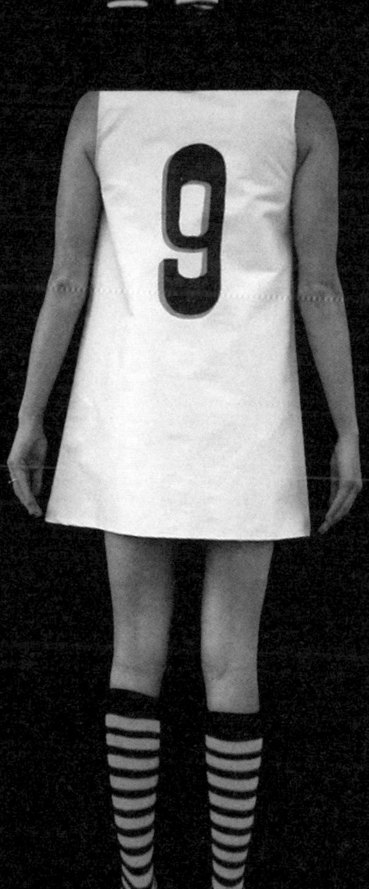
9

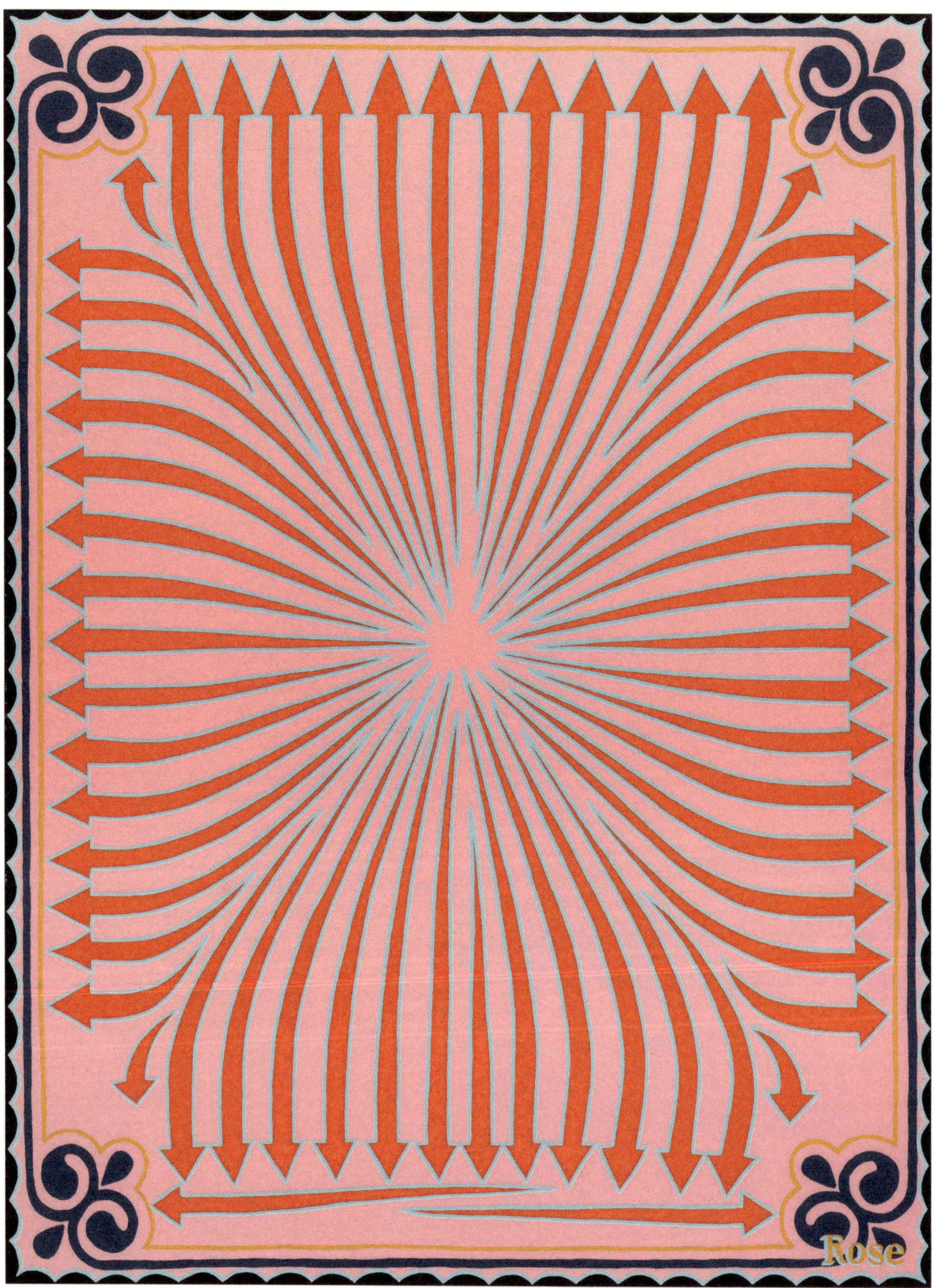
Rose

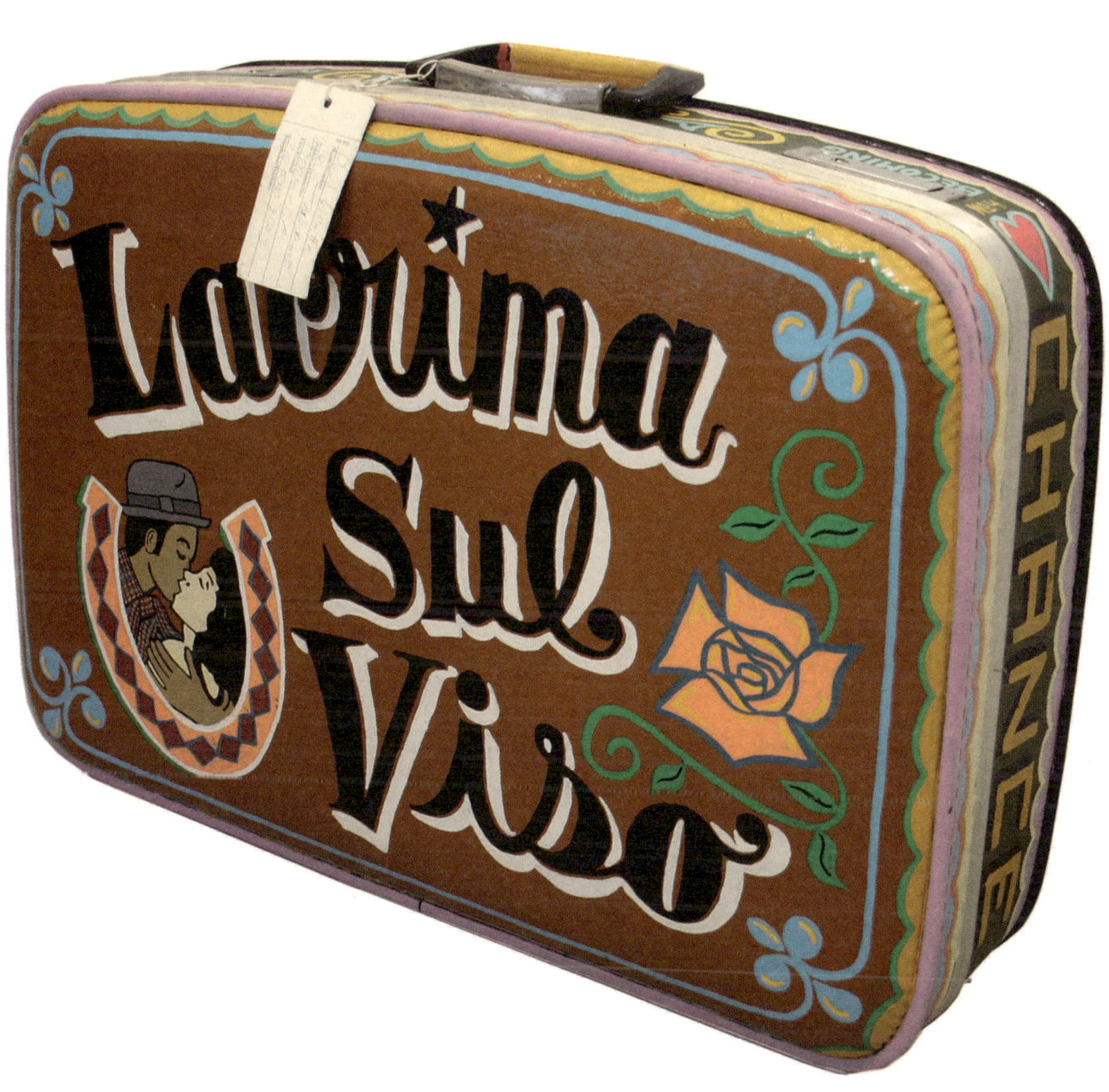
Lacrima
Sul
Viso
CHANCE

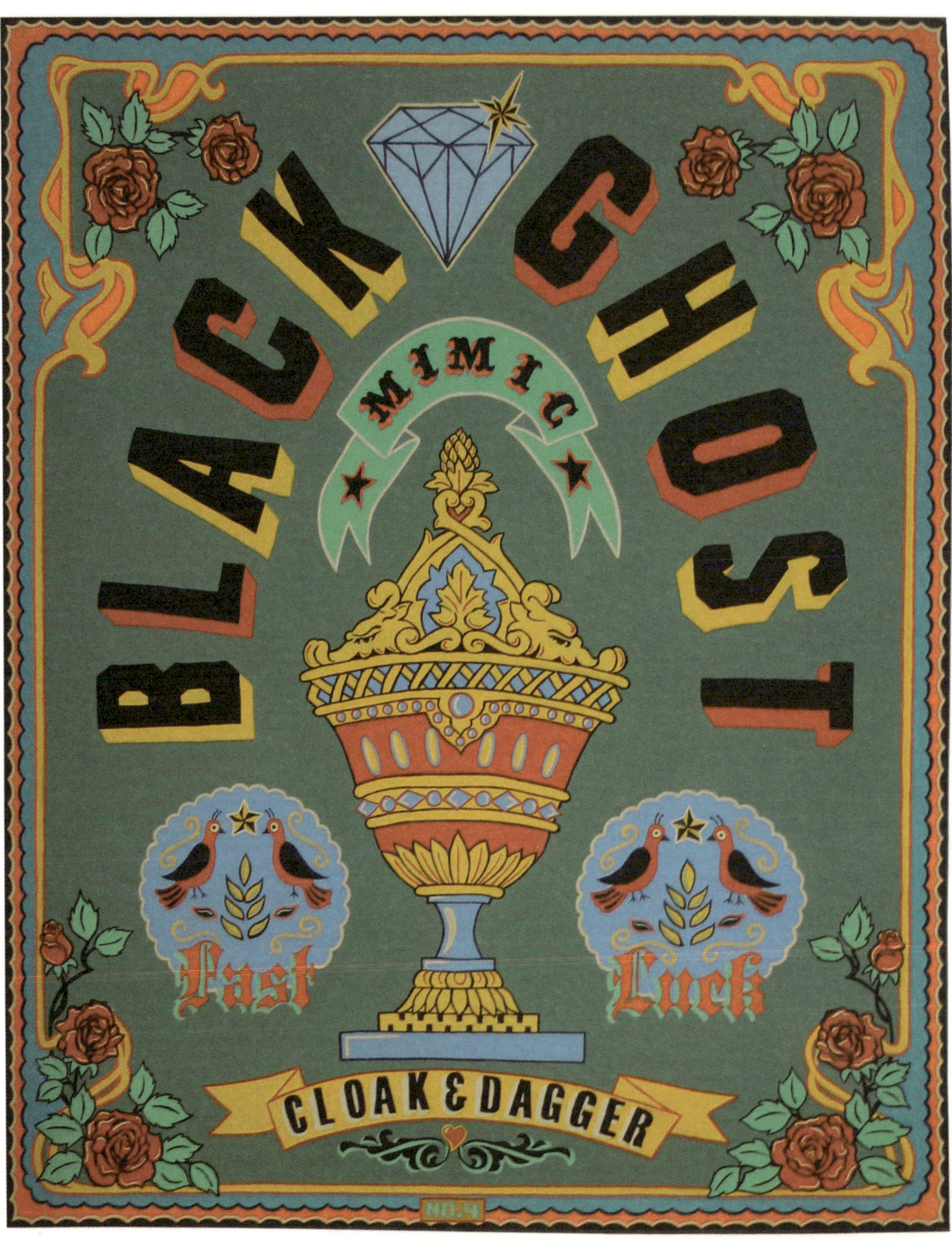
BLACK GHOST
MIMIC
Fast
Luck
CLOAK & DAGGER
NO. 4

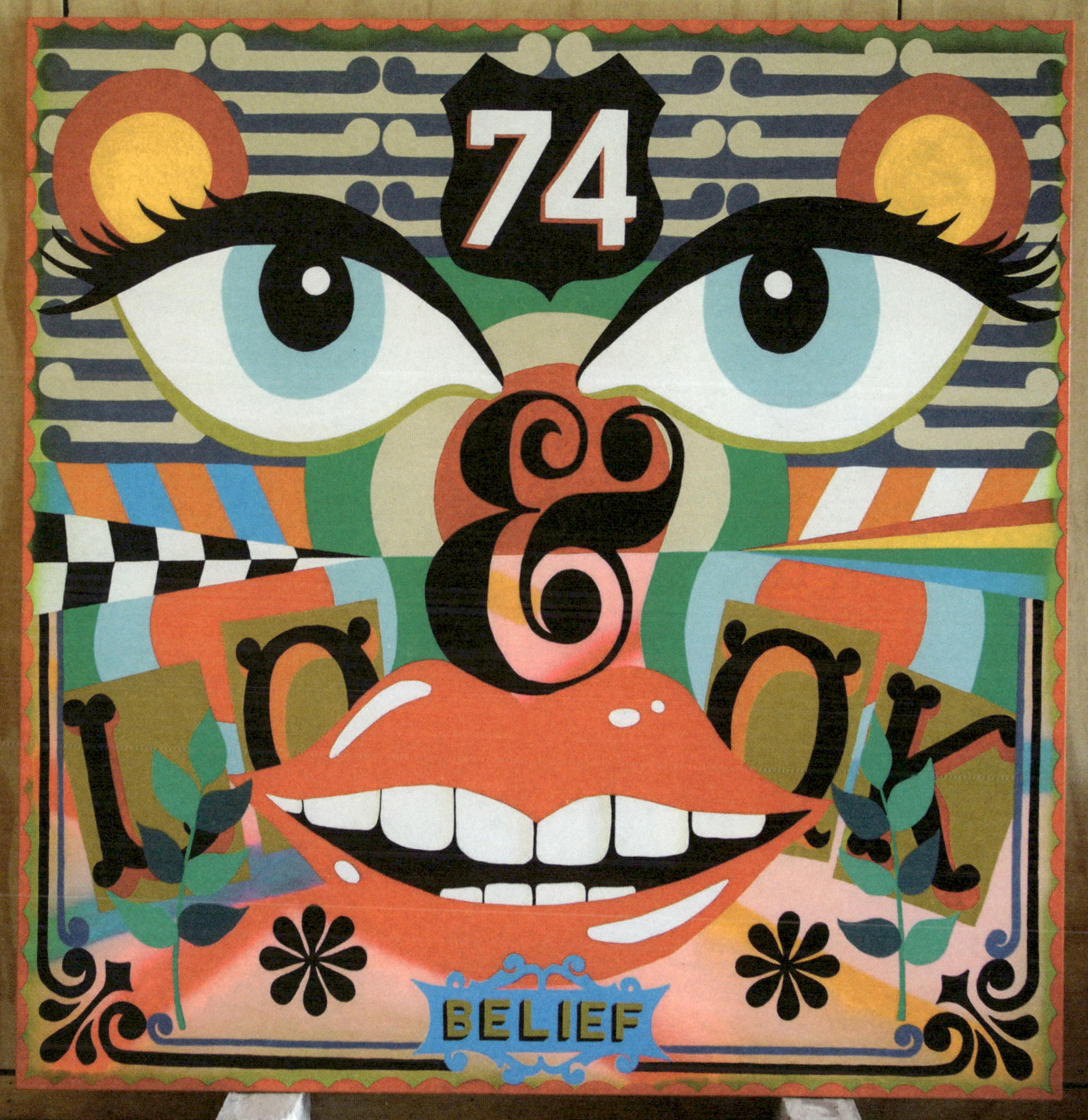
74
&
BELIEF

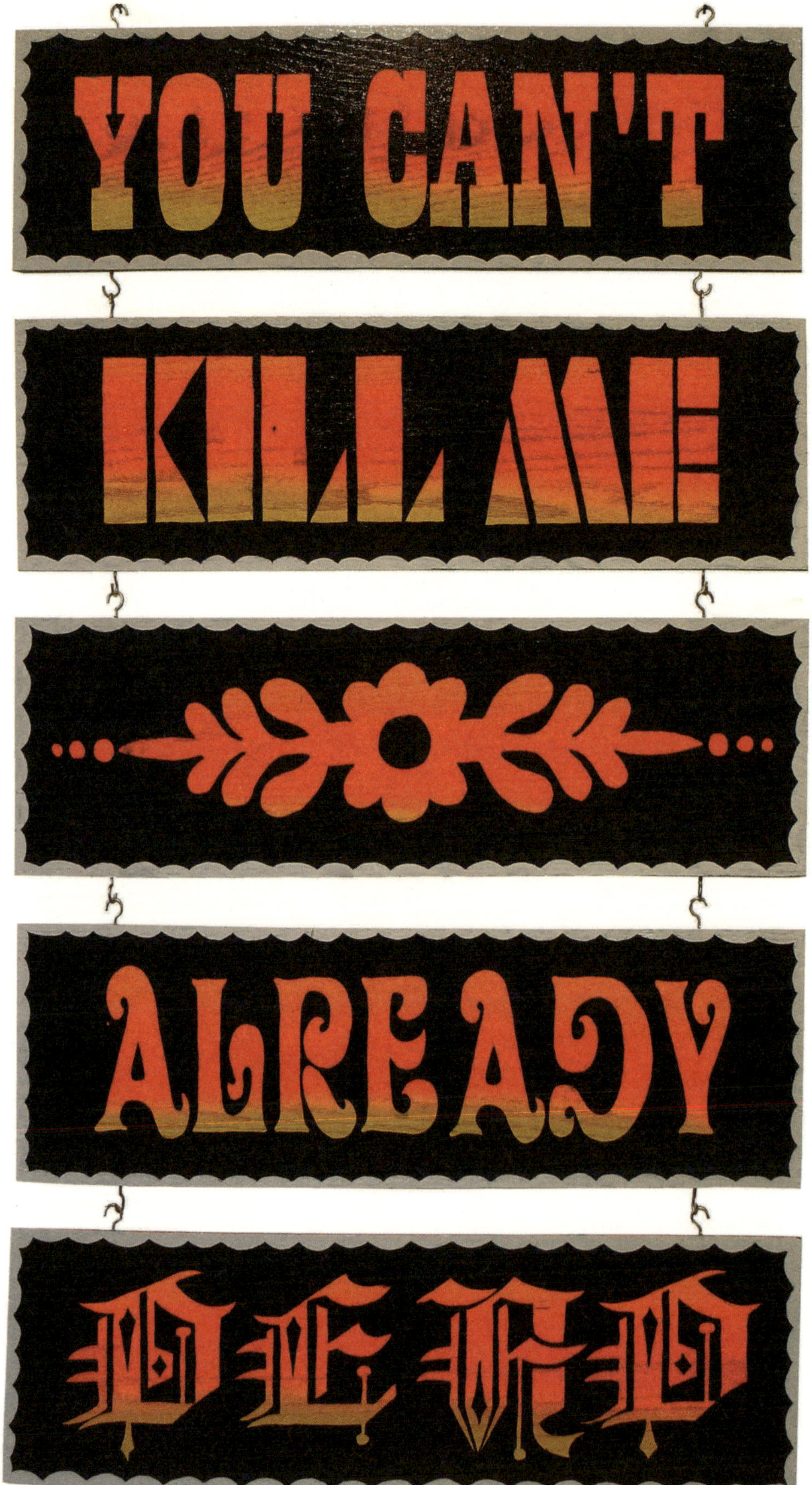

YOU CAN'T

KILL ME

ALREADY

DEAD

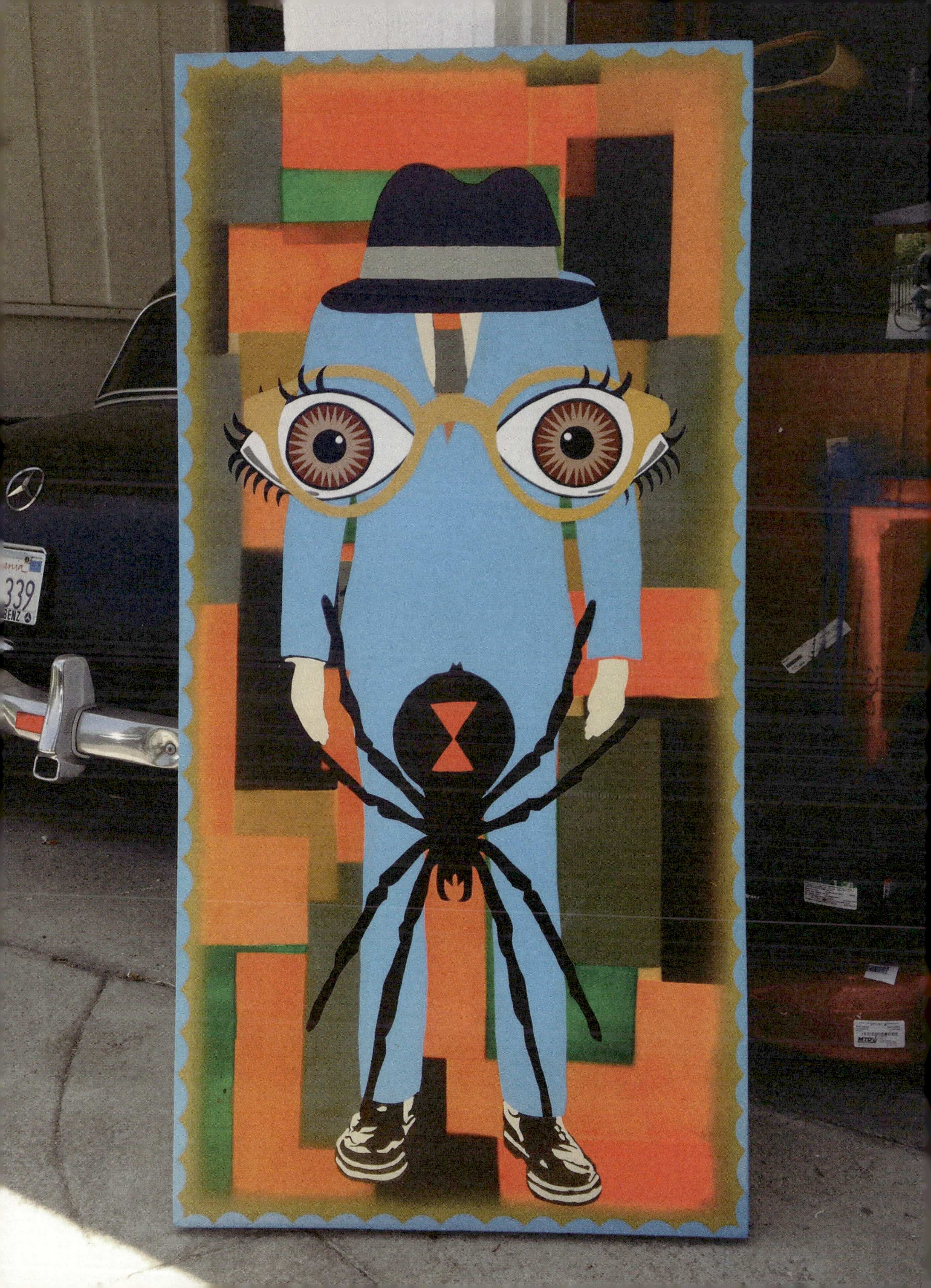

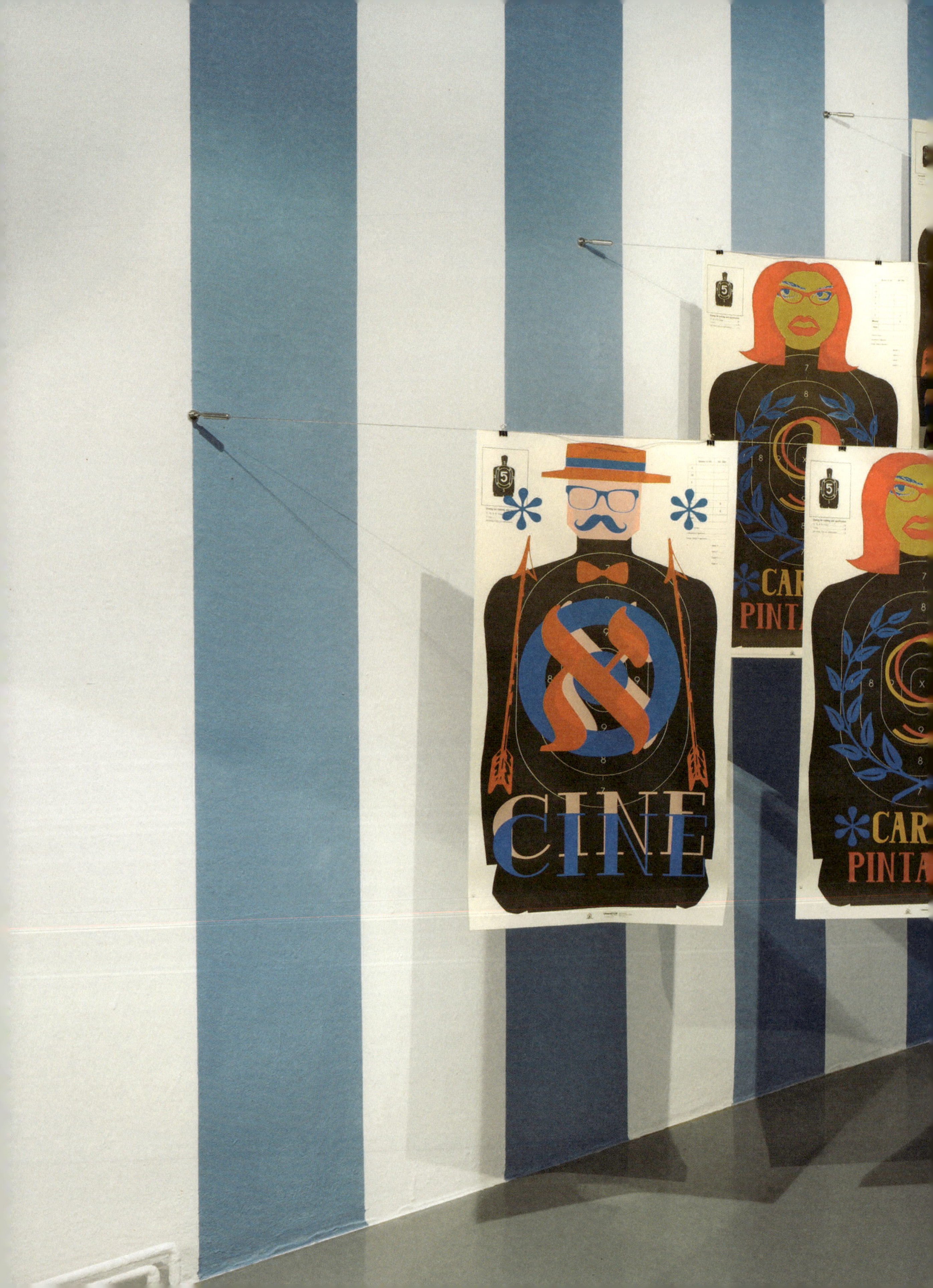
CINE
CINE

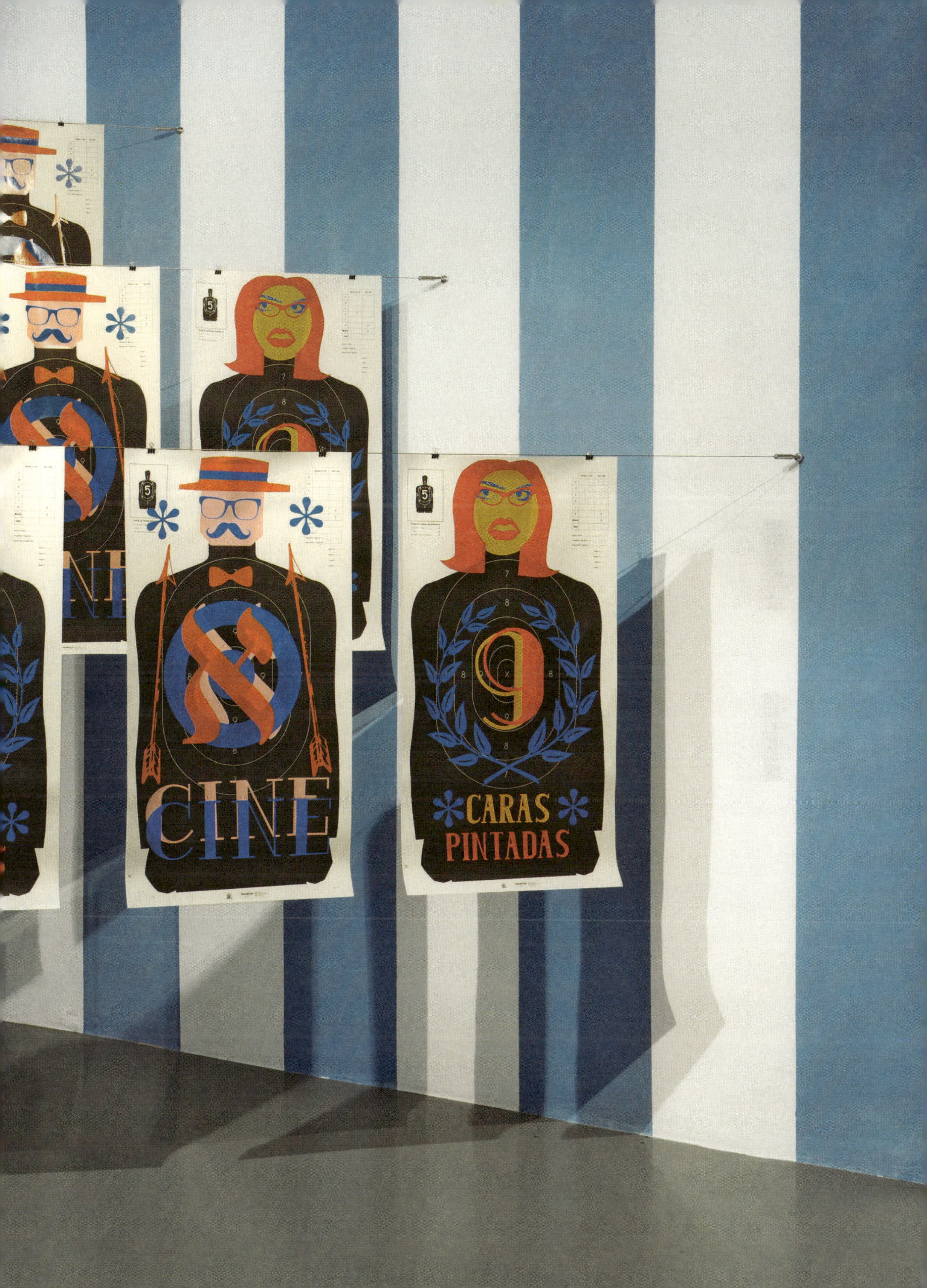
CINE
CARAS
PINTADAS

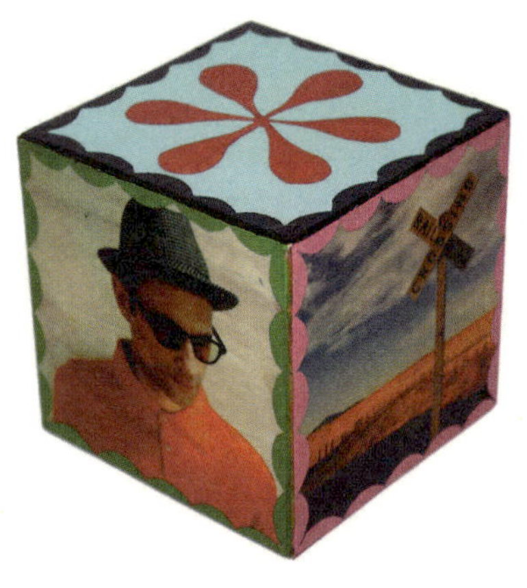

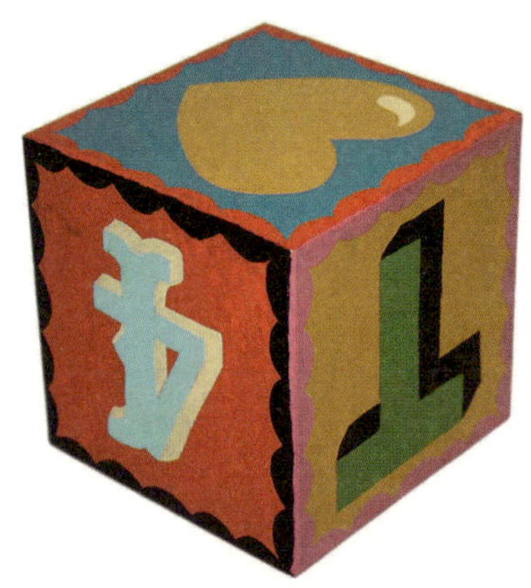

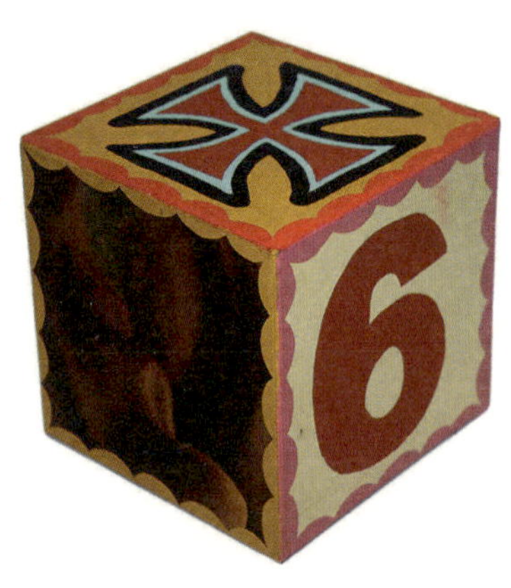

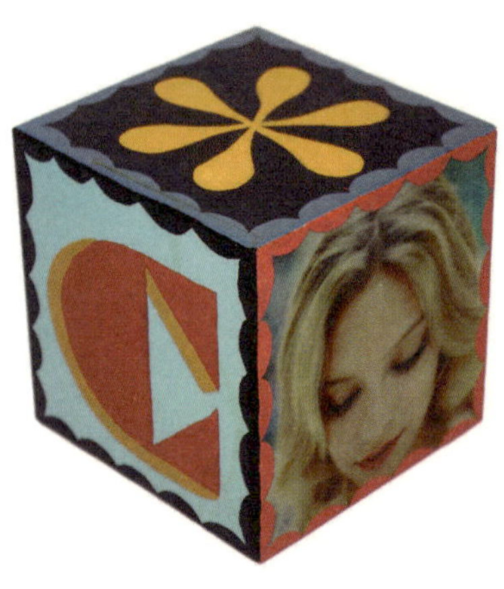

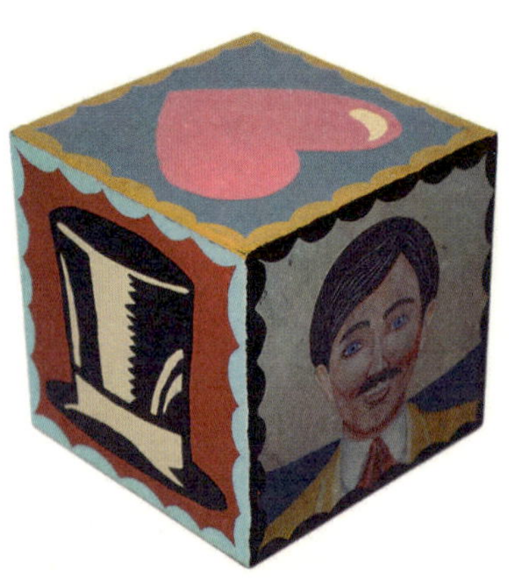

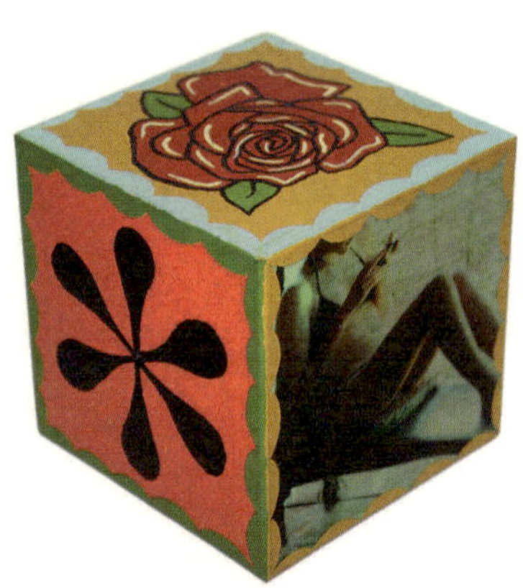

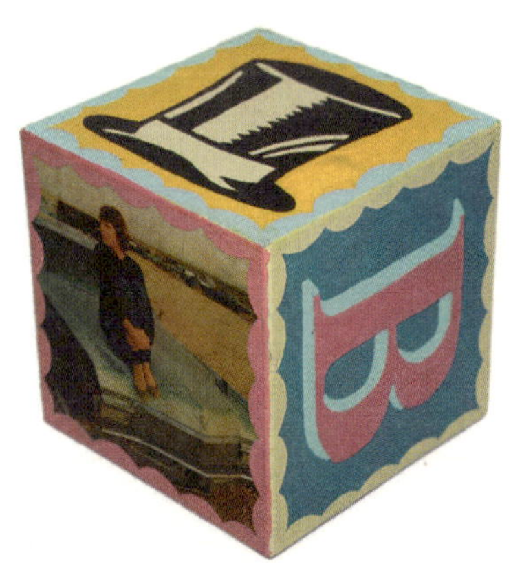

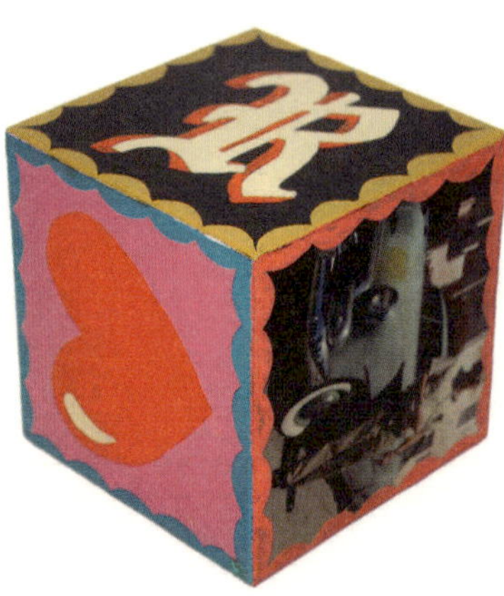

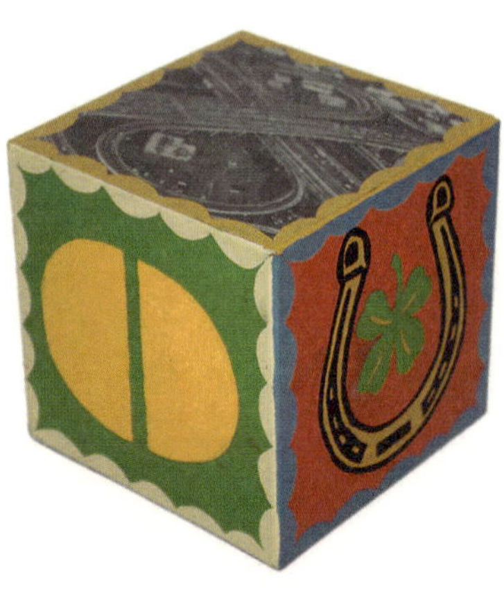

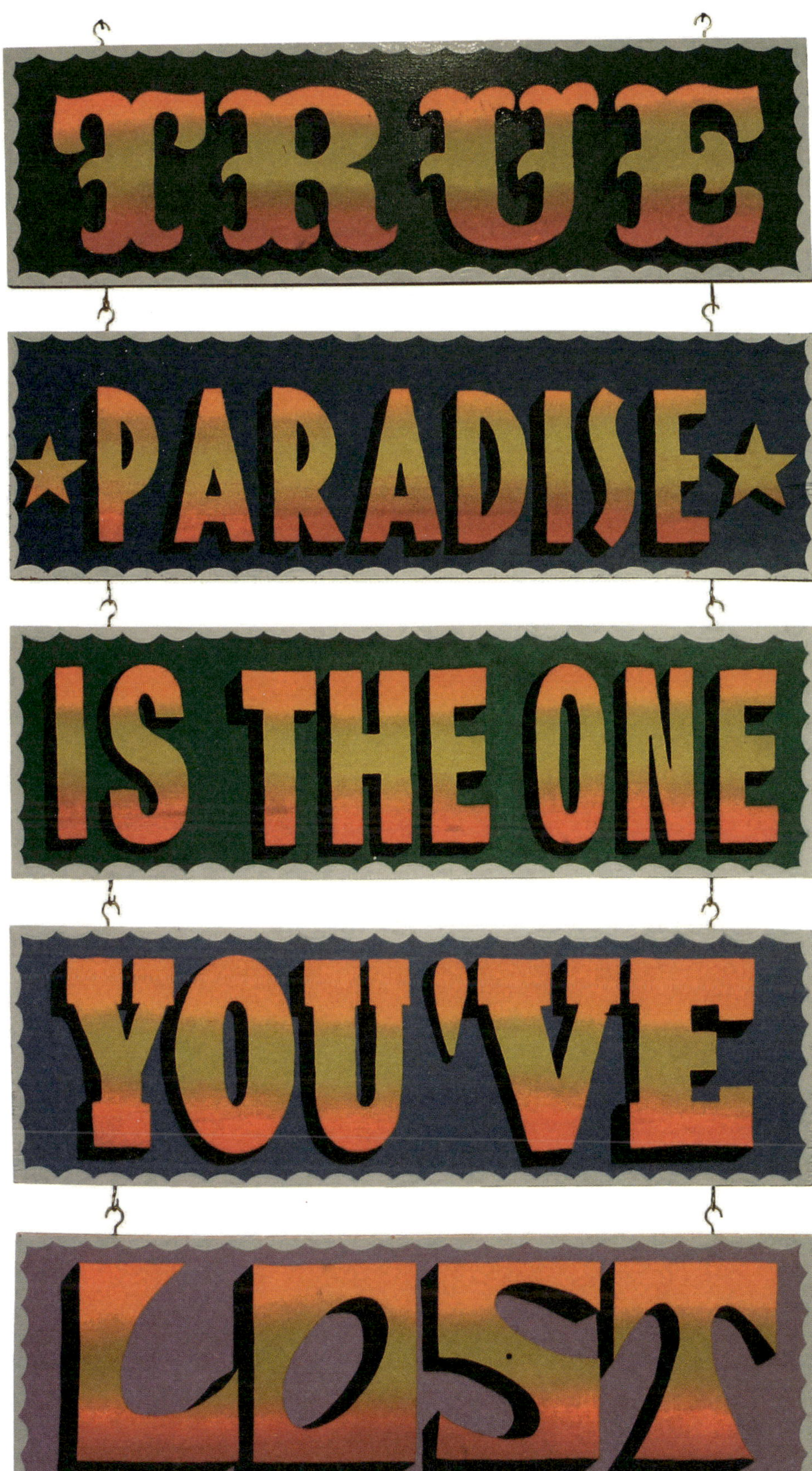
TRUE
PARADISE
IS THE ONE
YOU'VE
LOST

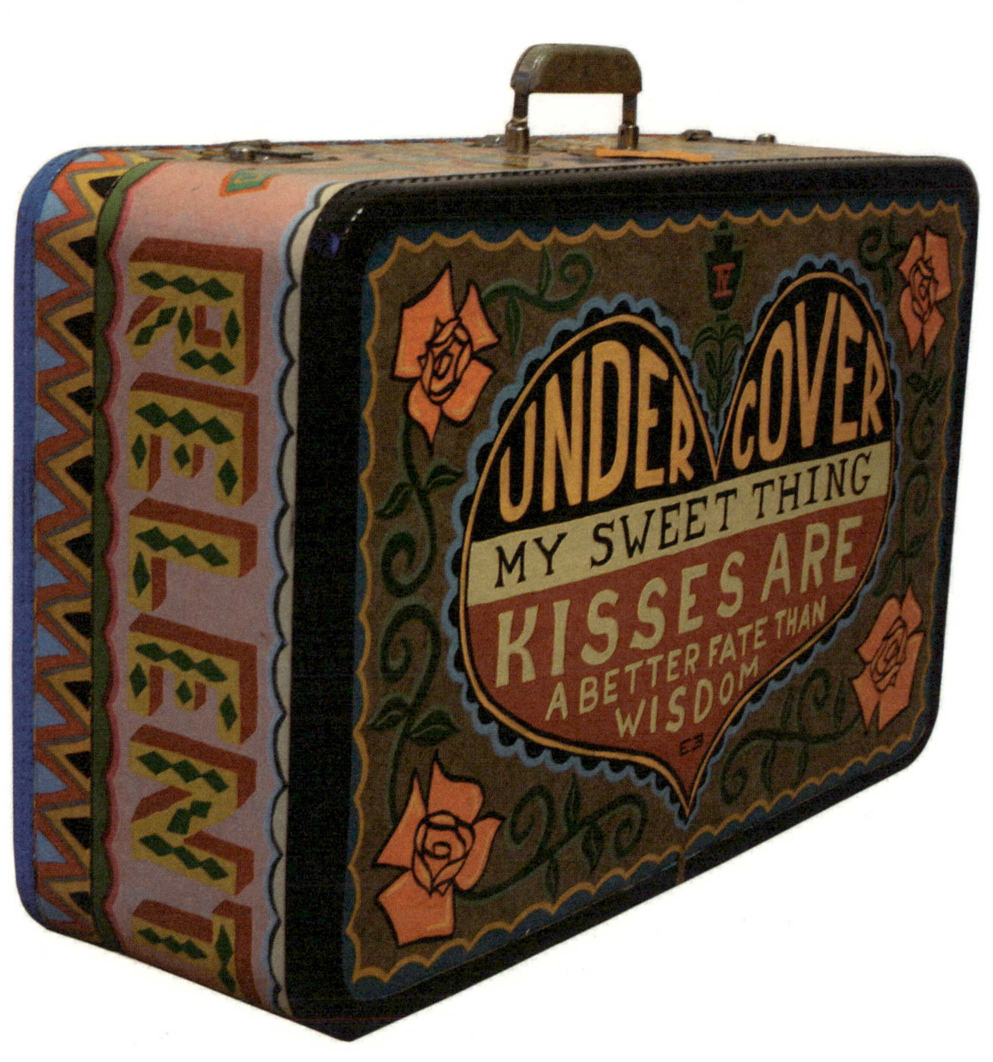
UNDER COVER
MY SWEET THING
KISSES ARE
A BETTER FATE THAN
WISDOM

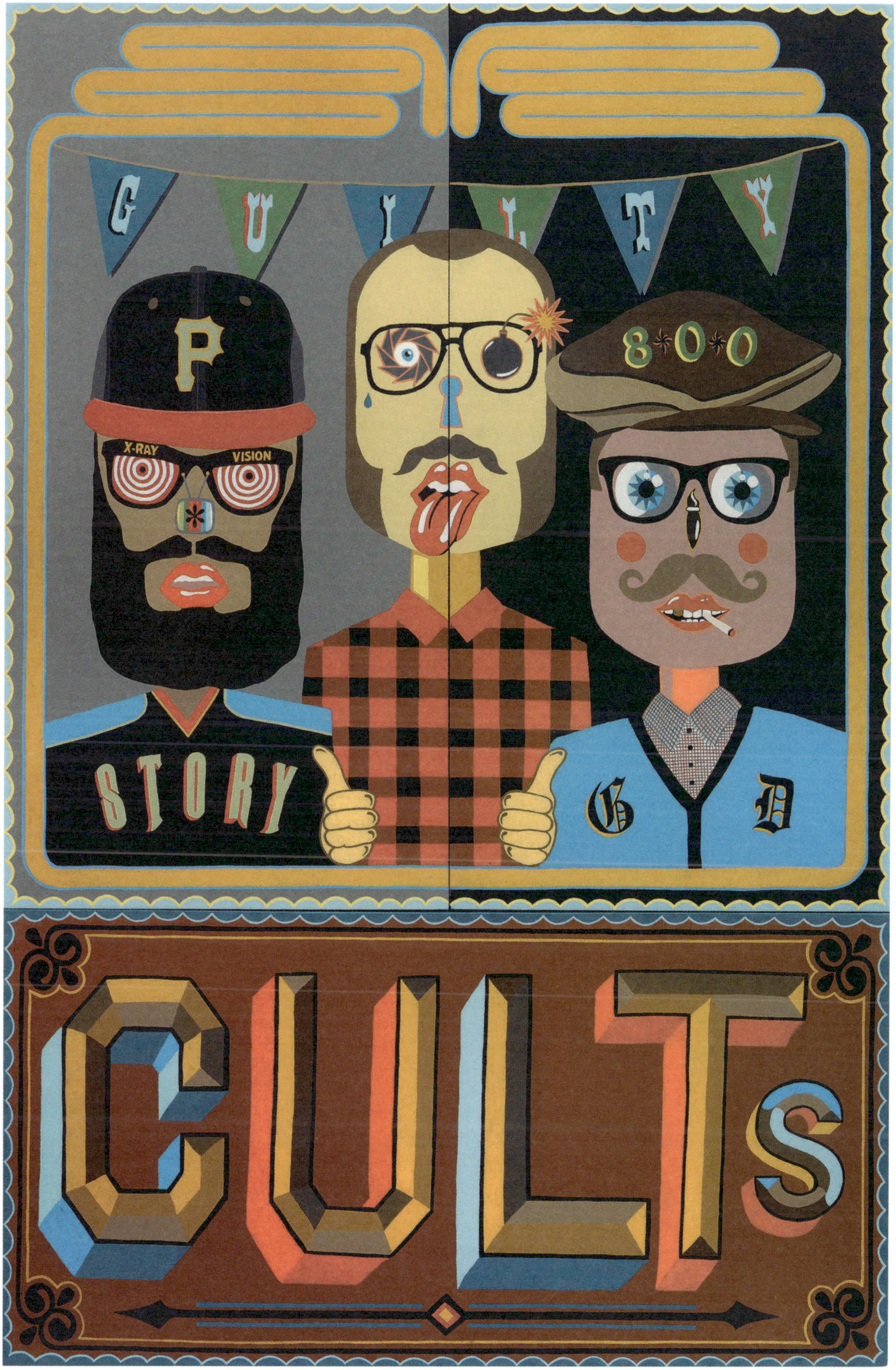

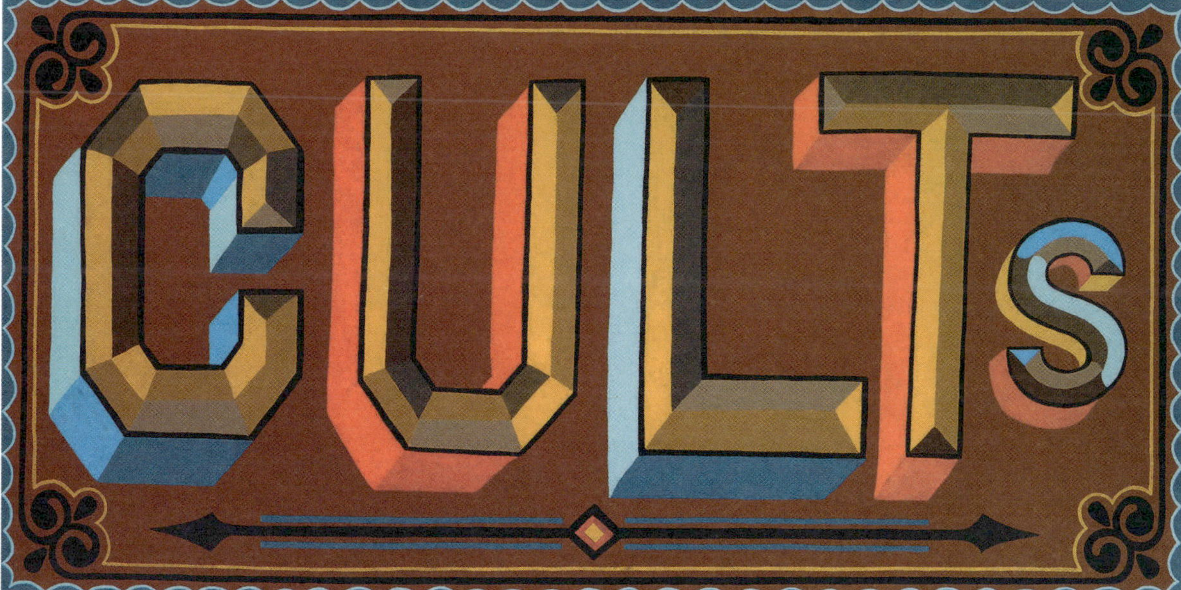
GUILTY
P
X-RAY VISION
800
STORY
G D
CULTs

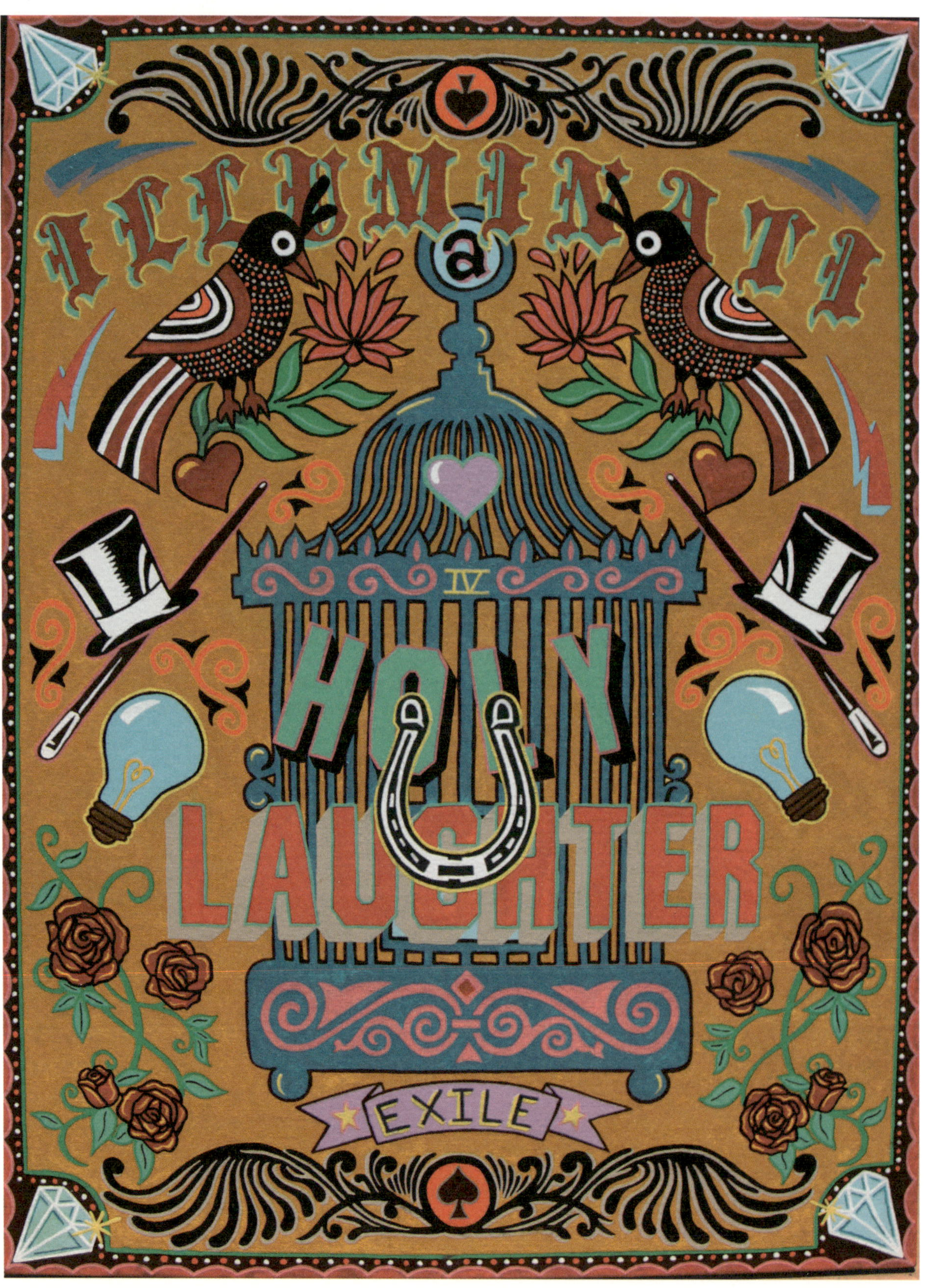
ILLUMINATI
a
IV
HOLY
LAUGHTER
EXILE

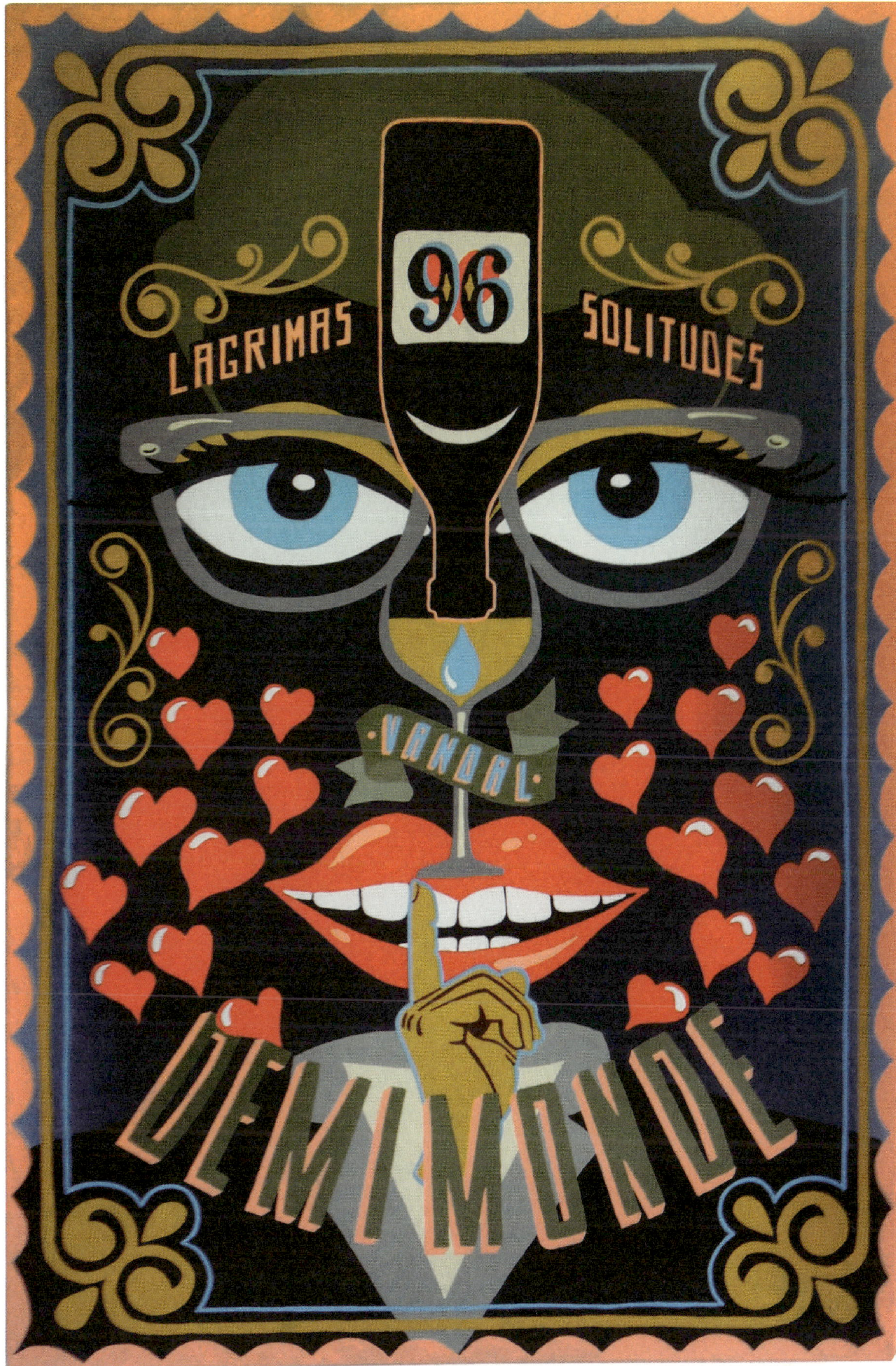
96
LAGRIMAS
SOLITUDES
VANDAL
DEMI MONDE

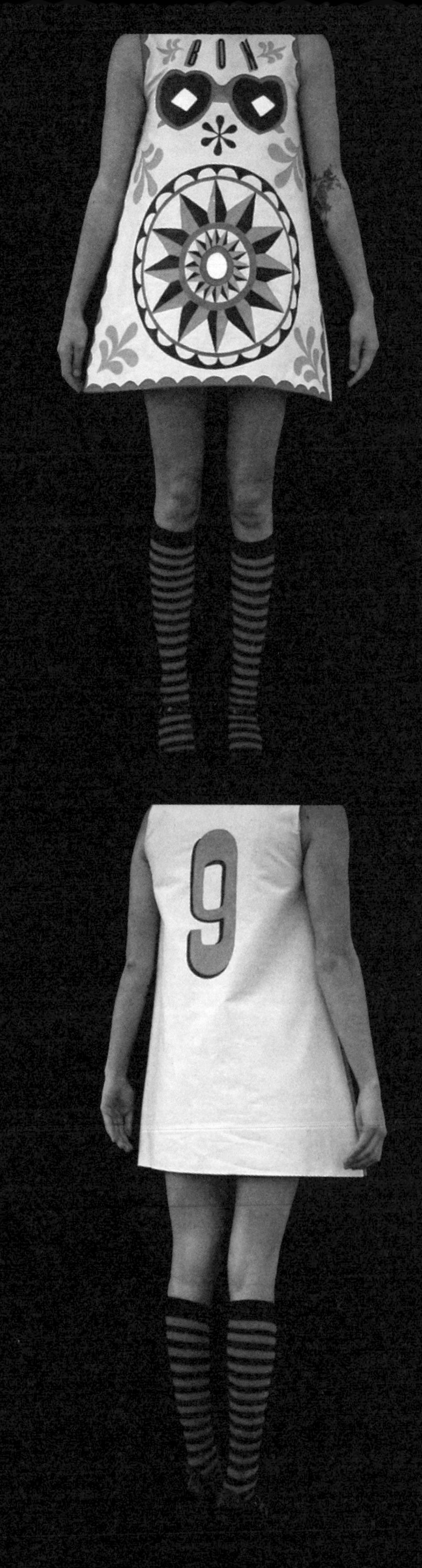
9

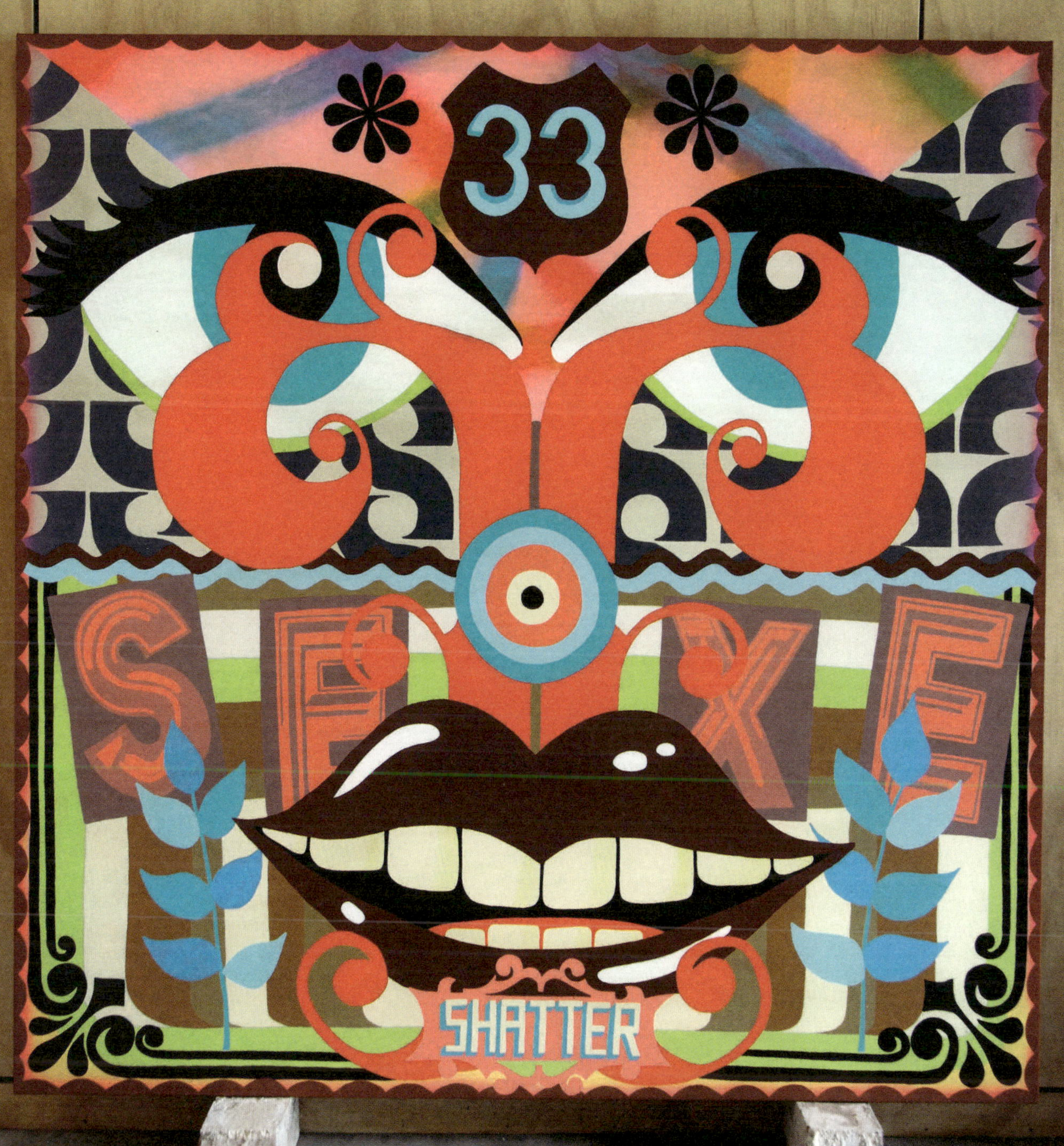
33
SEXE
SHATTER

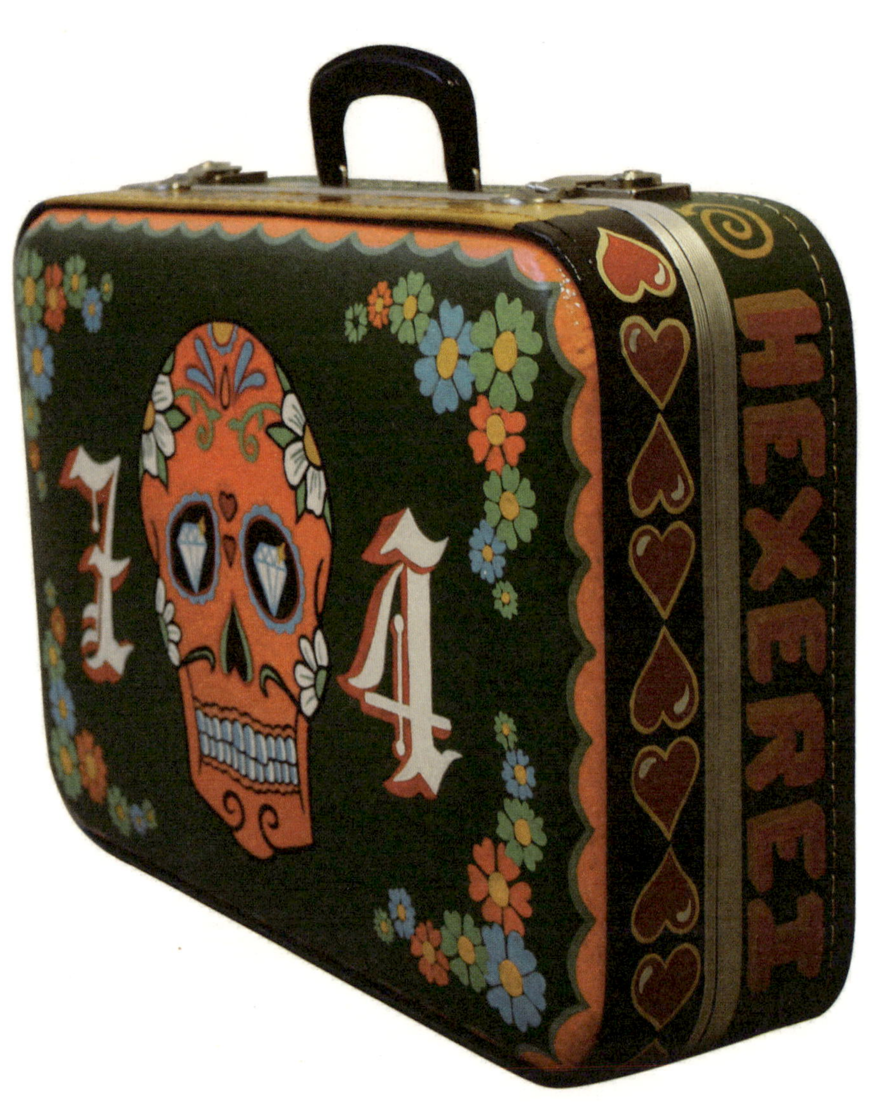
HEXEREI

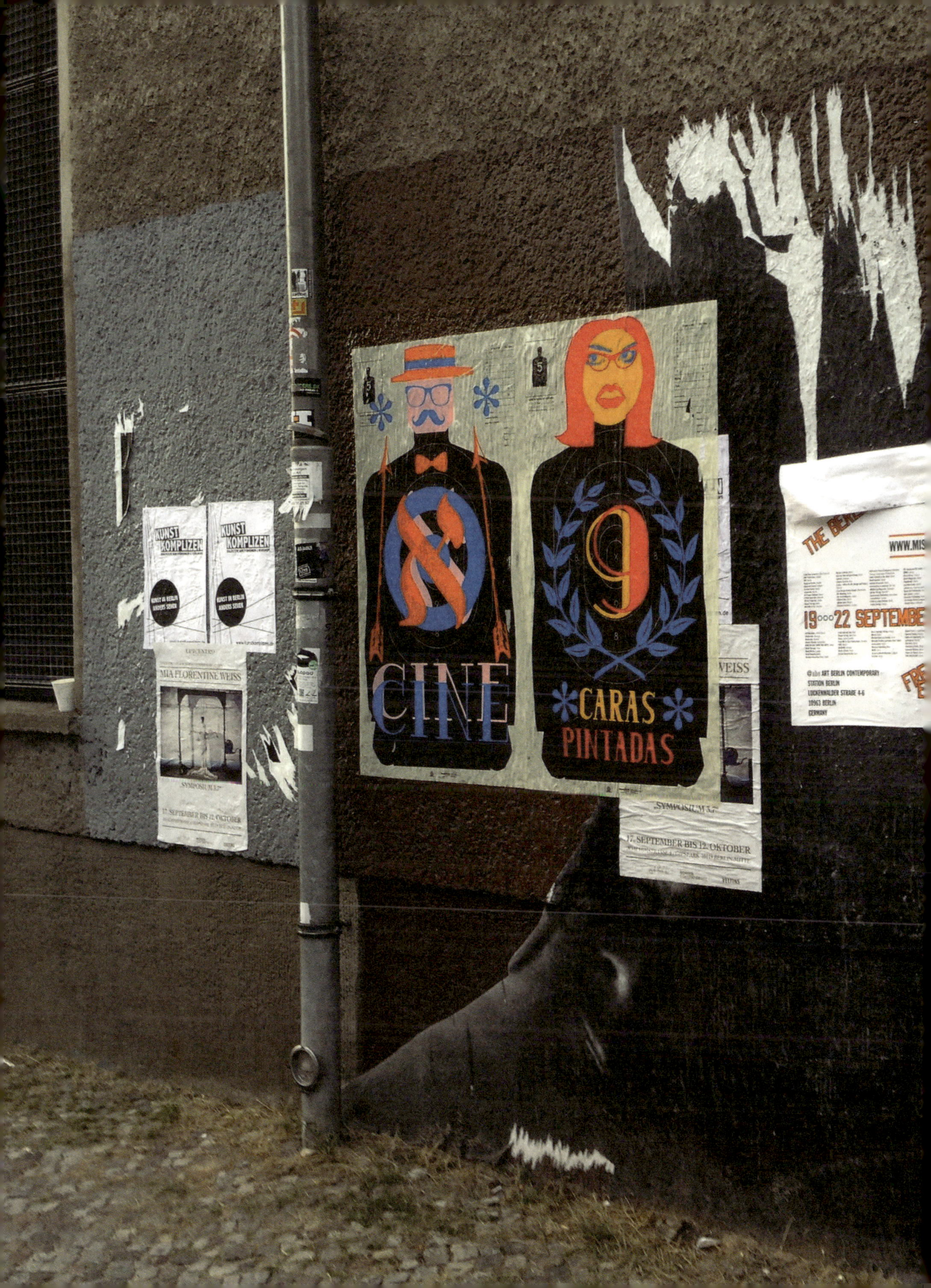
KUNST KOMPLIZEN
KUNST KOMPLIZEN
MIA FLORENTINE WEISS
17. SEPTEMBER BIS 12. OKTOBER
CINE
9
CARAS
PINTADAS
17. SEPTEMBER BIS 12. OKTOBER
19...22 SEPTEMBER
ART BERLIN CONTEMPORARY
STATION BERLIN
LUCKENWALDER STRASSE 4-6
10963 BERLIN
GERMANY

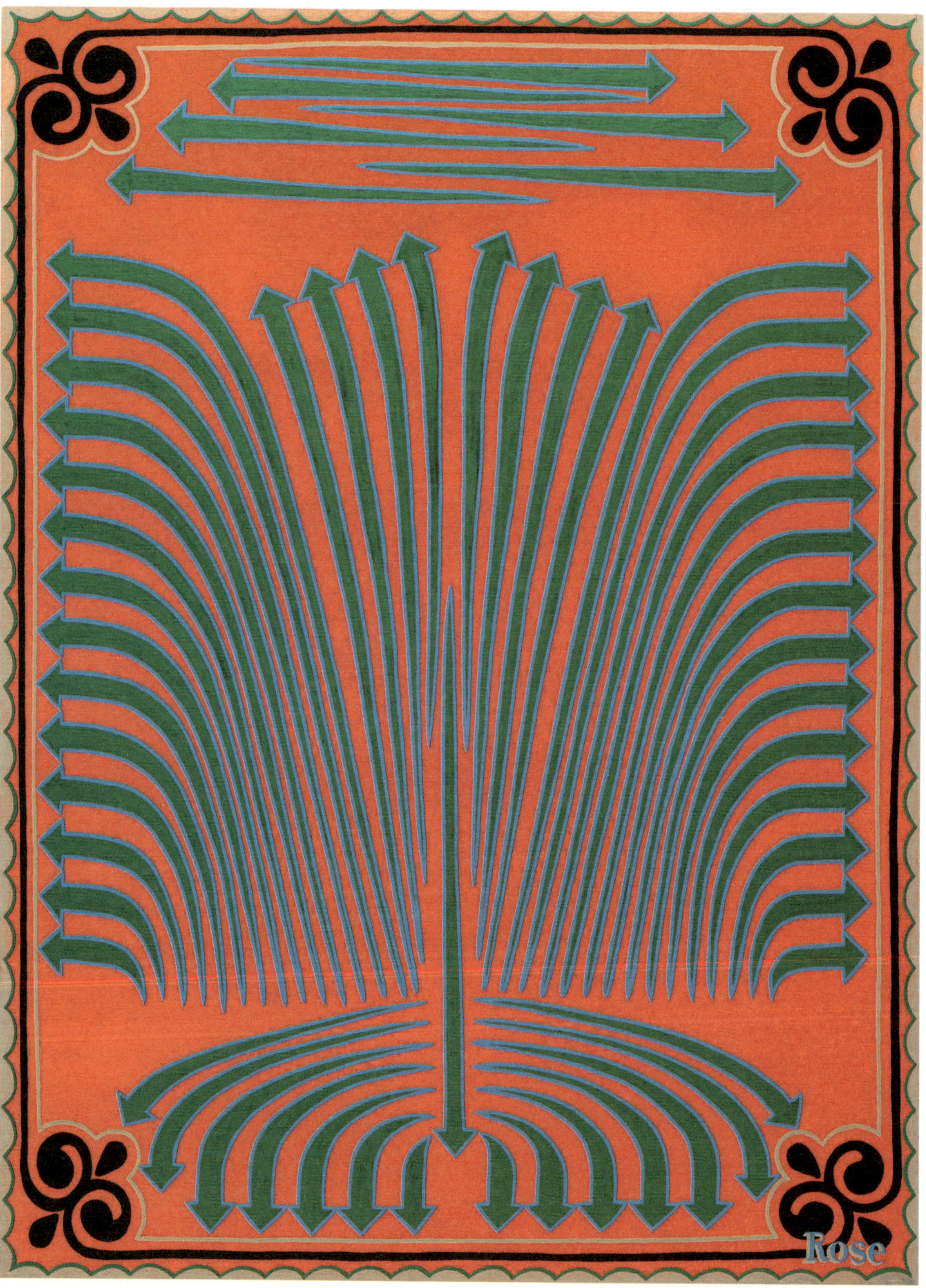
Rose

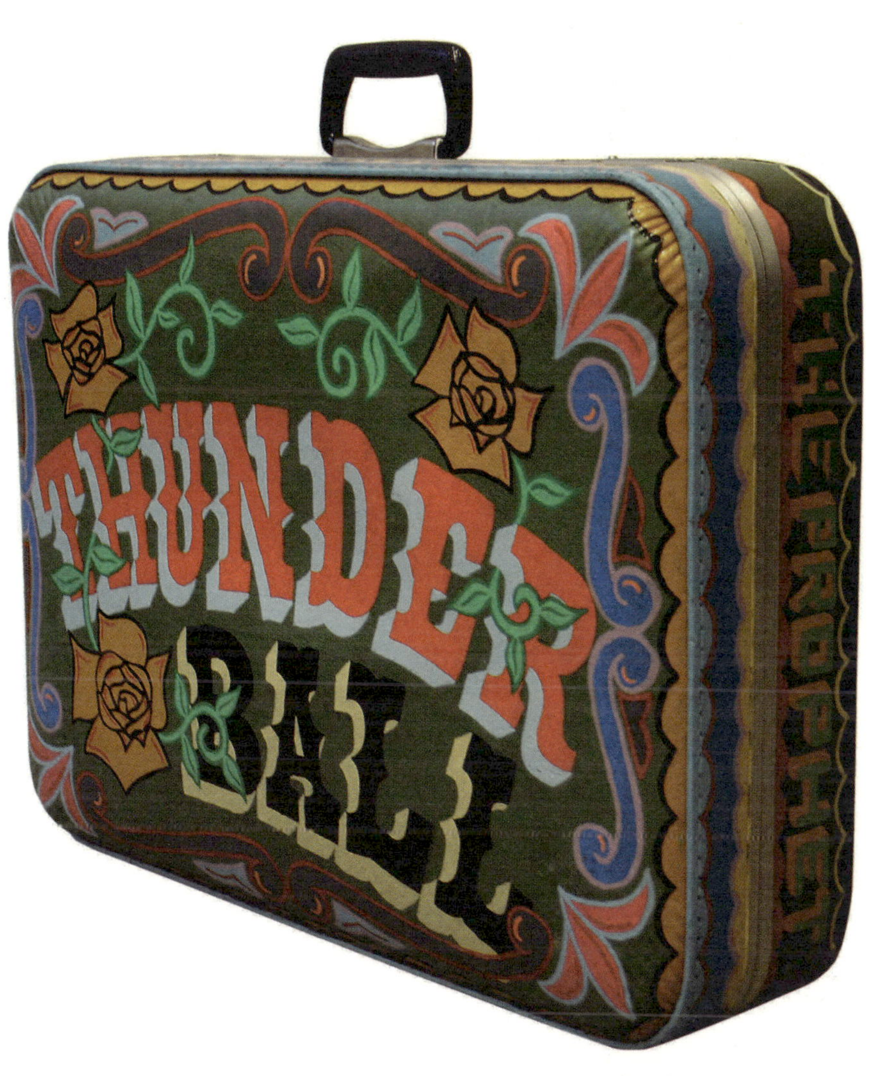
THUNDER
BALL
THE PROPHET

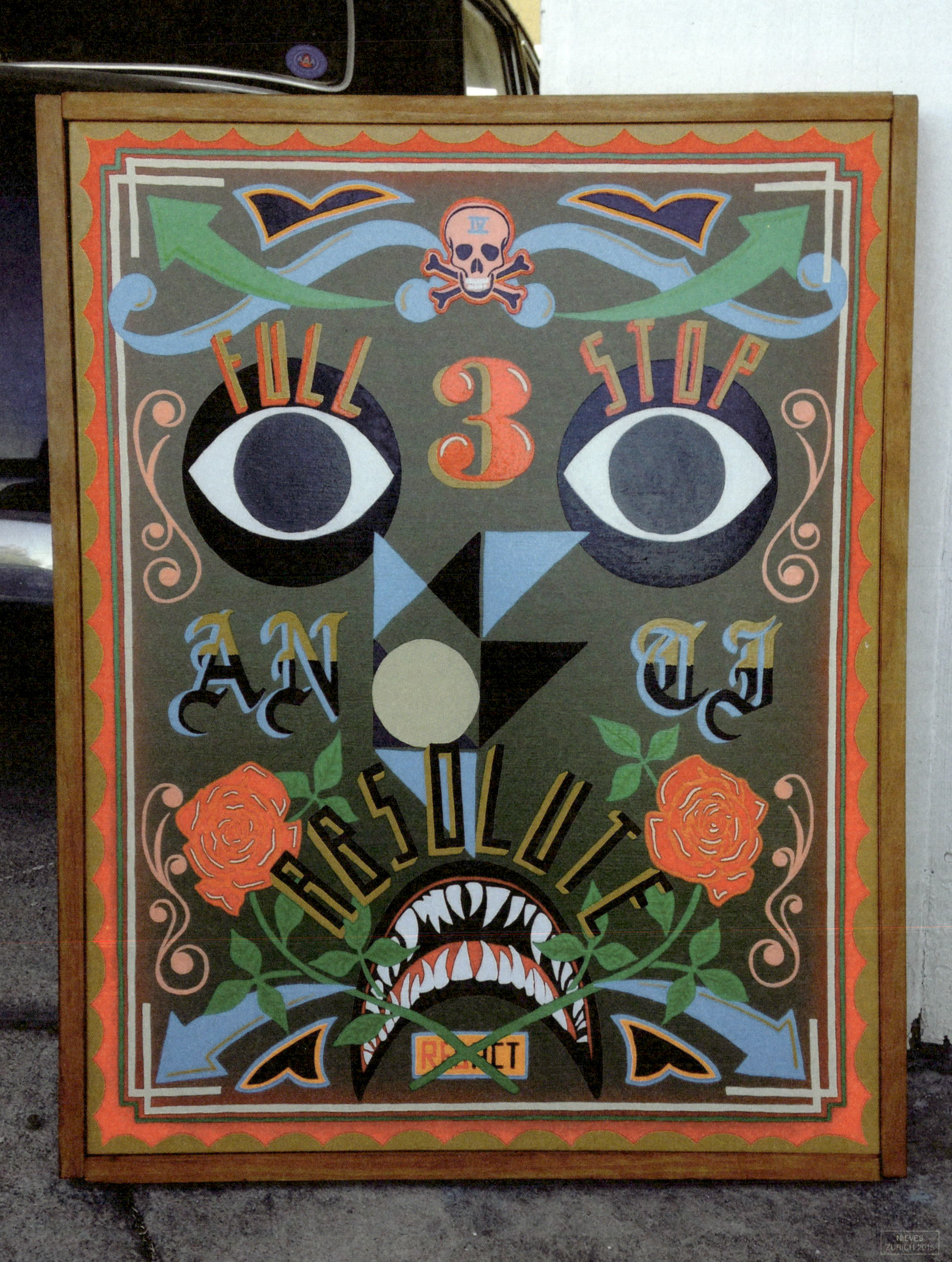

NIEVES
ZURICH 2015